ELIZABETH HOLMES AND THE THERANOS SCANDAL

The Rise and Spectacular Fall of Silicon Valley 's Most Ambitious Female Entrepreneur and Tech Prodigy Who Conned the World's Richest Investors

By

Cassandra T. Peters

TABLE OF CONTENT

Elizabeth Holmes, formerly renowned for her potential to transform the healthcare sector, is now the focal point of a riveting and contentious story in contemporary business history. As the founder and previous Chief Executive Officer of Theranos, a formerly renowned health technology corporation, Holmes attracted global attention with her aspiration to enhance the accessibility, efficiency, and affordability of blood testing. Characterized by her unique turtlenecks and unflinching self-assurance, Holmes emerged as an emblem of both Silicon

Valley's ingenuity and female business acumen.

Nevertheless, the perception of her has undergone a significant change, as the once-promising image has been completely destroyed. This has exposed allegations of fraudulent behavior, deceitful methods, and ultimately led to the bankruptcy of Theranos. As a result, Holmes has become the focus of intense scrutiny and legal actions.

This book extensively explores the scandal that profoundly impacted Silicon Valley and the global community. It examines Holmes's underlying motivations and traces her intricate path from a prodigious entrepreneur to the epicenter of a widely-publicized scandal.

CHAPTER ONE

Early Life of Elizabeth Holmes

Elizabeth Holmes was the founder and former chief executive officer of Theranos, an unsuccessful health technology firm located in Silicon Valley that promoted more affordable, non-intrusive blood testing. Following the company's valuation surpassing $9 billion, multiple reports surfaced indicating that Holmes' technology was flawed and a significant number of the 7.5 million tests conducted may have yielded erroneous results. Holmes and former Theranos Chief Operating Officer Ramesh "Sunny" Balwani were formally accused in June 2018 of 11 federal crimes, which encompassed wire fraud and a conspiracy to engage in wire fraud.

Background and Academic Training

Elizabeth Anne Holmes, born on February 3, 1984, in Washington, is the daughter of Noel, a former Capitol Hill committee staffer, and Christian, who held positions in various governmental agencies, including the United States Agency for International Development (USAID). Holmes' family relocated from Washington to Houston during his early years.

Holmes initiated her entrepreneurial journey at a young age, driven by her teenage fascination with computer programming. This passion prompted her to establish a company that specialized in providing coding translation software to Chinese institutions. In addition, she commenced her study of Mandarin Chinese at an early age, enabling her to partake in a sequence of college-level courses while still in high school.

In 2002, she enrolled at Stanford University to pursue a degree in chemical engineering. During her time there, she collaborated with Channing Robertson, who was a dean at the university and later became one of the initial board members of Theranos. Her phobia of needles hindered her from pursuing a career in the medical field, although it did not deter her from establishing Theranos. The businesswoman established her company the year before her graduation from Stanford University's chemical engineering department.

Holmes' motivation for establishing her company arose from a summer internship in 2002 at the Genome Institute of Singapore. from this internship, she engaged in research and testing related to Severe Acute Respiratory Syndrome (SARS). During his sabbatical from Stanford, Holmes conducted research at the Genome Institute of Singapore, focusing on the detection of the SARS virus using a computer processor. Her interest in medical device invention was sparked by her recognition of the constraints of existing diagnostic and therapeutic evaluation techniques. Holmes went back to Stanford and created a device that could be connected to a patient in order to assess the effectiveness of a treatment. This was done by comparing the chemical marker parameters produced by an affected area with those of the therapeutic substance.

CHAPTER TWO

The Birth of Theranos

In 2003, she obtained a U.S. patent for her original concept of a drug delivery system. This system was designed to perform multiple functions within a single tiny patch, including drug administration, effectiveness testing, and dosage adjustment.

At the age of 19, Holmes dropped out from Stanford University and utilized her college tuition funds as initial capital to establish a company named Real-Time Cures. In the subsequent years,

Holmes redirected her attention towards developing an innovative method of blood analysis, asserting that it was derived from her personal aversion to needles. The corporation underwent a rebranding process and adopted the name Theranos, which is a combination of the term "treatment" and "diagnostic."

Theranos promptly asserted that they had created multiple exclusive techniques. One obviated the necessity of gathering blood samples by conventional needles, opting instead for a finger prick that gathered minuscule quantities of blood into a diminutive tube known as a "nanotainer." Another device was a laboratory apparatus capable of conducting numerous tests on a little quantity of blood, detecting diseases such as diabetes, cancer, and heart disease. Theranos advocated for new legislation in multiple states that would permit the administration of tests without requiring a doctor's prescription. Both technologies have the potential to significantly transform the diagnostics sector, which was estimated to be worth between $52–57 billion globally in the early 2010s. Theranos provided these blood tests at a substantially reduced price compared to conventional testing facilities and hospitals. While certain traditional tests may have had a price tag of several hundred dollars, Theranos provided them at a cost of less than $5 and guaranteed quicker outcomes.

Laboratory data served as a crucial resource for clinicians to inform and enable patients in making healthcare decisions. Theranos's approach asserted that a minute sample (a few drops from a fingerprick) was adequate for the company's diagnostic tests, proving to be notably less agonizing and costly compared to traditional testing methods. Holmes clandestinely expanded Theranos between 2003 and 2014 by enlisting investors, building infrastructure, and formulating exclusive techniques. Walgreen Co., with a nationwide presence of more than 8,000 stores in the United States, declared a collaboration with Theranos in 2013 to create wellness centers within its pharmacies.

The Centers for Medicare & Medicaid Services (CMS), the governmental entity tasked with overseeing medical laboratories, granted certification to Theranos in 2014 following the completion of more than 200 diagnostic tests. In late 2015, Theranos's exclusive technology and its main medical testing gadget, the Edison, became the center of criticism following a series of articles by journalists.

From 2014 to 2015, Elizabeth Holmes was featured on the front covers of seven prominent magazines, consistently portrayed with a uniform style and pose: wearing a black turtleneck, projecting a commanding gaze, and with her blonde hair swept back. She fostered a remarkable following based on her personal charm and charisma, which is frequently seen as a significant factor in Theranos' appeal to its influential board members and wealthy investors.

Reportedly, she purportedly modulated her voice to gain credibility in her predominantly male field.

Holmes successfully assembled a powerful alliance of supporters. Channing Robertson, a professor at Stanford, was one of her earliest and most prominent supporters. Following Holmes' completion of her internship at Robertson's lab, he assumed the role of her mentor and became the company's inaugural board member. The bioengineering specialist received a generous compensation to enhance the company's credibility among the scientific community. He dedicated a significant amount of effort to addressing the opponents of Holmes and Theranos who had expressed serious reservations about the technology. It is uncertain whether Robertson was cognizant of the issues.

CHAPTER THREE

Theranos Board of Directors

In 2011, George Shultz encountered Holmes and subsequently became a member of the Theranos board of directors. Notable individuals such as Henry Kissinger and William Perry, who served as Secretaries of State, along with Jim Mattis and Richard Kovacevich, who served as Secretaries of Defense, and Richard Kovacevich, the former CEO of Wells Fargo Bank, were all added to the board with his help in subsequent years. The Walton family, the first owners of Walmart, donated $150 million to Holmes's company. All individuals who had made investments in Theranos incurred financial losses upon its failure.

In 2009, Holmes collaborated with Ramesh "Sunny" Balwani, a software developer who lacked expertise in healthcare or medicine but had previously established and sold a technology company. He assumed the role of president and chief operational officer at Theranos, overseeing its daily operations. He lacked proficiency in biology and had no prior experience in the initial stages of a technology company's startup. The laboratory personnel quickly discerned his lack of familiarity with the methods and technologies employed in the facility. As a result of his volatile temperament, Balwani quickly established himself as an "enforcer" within the group.

 The staff and board of directors were kept unaware of Holmes' clandestine romantic involvement with Balwani. Despite the company's reluctance to disclose its methods and technology, citing concerns about potential competitors, it successfully secured several profitable agreements. Notably, it partnered with Walgreens to introduce

Theranos labs in almost 50 of their stores, with intentions to expand to thousands more. The company also asserted its collaboration with the U.S. Department of Defense and prominent pharmaceutical companies such as Pfizer and GlaxoSmithKline, although subsequent investigations refuted these assertions. The intended $350 million agreement with Safeway was abandoned due to the emergence of allegations against the corporation.

In 2014, Theranos had a valuation of $9 billion. As a result, Holmes, who was 30 years old and possessed a 50 percent stake in the company, became the youngest female billionaire who had achieved success by her own efforts. By 2015, her net worth had surged to $4.7 billion, primarily due to her significant investment in Theranos stock.

CHAPTER FOUR

The Meteoric Rise and Fall of Elizabeth Holmes

As her company gained significant attention, so did Holmes. She was prominently showcased in numerous newspaper and magazine profiles. Holmes, who often wore black attire, including a mock turtleneck, was frequently likened to the innovative Apple cofounder Steve Jobs, a similarity that Holmes deliberately fostered. Holmes diligently labored every day of the week and asserted that she had never indulged in a vacation, qualities she fervently instilled in her staff. Her deep-pitched voice, which was one of her most prominent characteristics, received attention and was analyzed by the media. Numerous reports observed that she intentionally lowered her voice, potentially as a strategy to command respect in the predominantly male environment of Silicon Valley.

Laboratory personnel soon informed their superiors about the issues with the "Edison" and recorded them in error reports. The organization's management ignored these advices. The company's test trials were subjected to data filtering to eliminate any erroneous information, and thereafter analyzed instead of focusing on finding a solution. The decision was made to ignore the erroneous findings. Reportedly, Balwani, who was Holmes' associate, applied pressure on staff members who were dubious or critical.

Former Theranos employees depicted the company's workplace atmosphere as marked by deceit, psychological distress, and suspicion. Holmes purportedly deceived her colleagues, even on insignificant matters, by falsely claiming in emails that she was absent from the office while she was actually present at her desk just a few feet away. Several employees either resigned or were dismissed due to their extensive criticism and relentless questioning.

The Whistleblowers

Tyler Shultz, the individual who exposed wrongdoing, commenced his employment at Theranos in 2013, and he displayed unwavering support for Holmes' objective right from the beginning and was the grandson of one of the board members in Theranos George Shultz.

Upon being awarded a permanent position on the diagnostic team, he promptly encountered difficulties with the examination outcomes. The department of internal statistics persisted in recording reports notwithstanding the presence of inaccuracies and manipulation of the data. Shultz noted that there was a lack of clear understanding of the functioning of "Edison" among individuals. Entry to the laboratory, where the machines were installed, was limited to authorized personnel, including the investigators. This was because Theranos did not supply the devices necessary for doing blood tests at that particular site. Erika Cheung, a laboratory assistant who was employed in the laboratory, joined the company as a result of being motivated by Holmes' desire. Cheung worked in the Theranos laboratory for a duration of six months, spanning from 2013 to 2014, until she became aware that erroneous test results had been deleted. Standard testing refuted her assertion of a vitamin D insufficiency, however, when she examined her own blood using a Theranos device, the findings suggested otherwise. She alerted Balwani to the difficulties, however, he doubted her expertise. Cheung opted to resign from the organization after completing six months of employment due to her profound apprehension regarding its future prospects. Subsequently, Theranos initiated a campaign of harassment against Cheung by hiring and deploying private detectives to pursue her. Subsequently, she revealed her intense fear and surveillance, prompting her to move several times and acquire a prepaid phone to safeguard her phone conversations from potential eavesdropping or recording.

Shultz also highlighted the challenges inside the company. He endeavored to engage in a conversation with Holmes, although his concerns were not regarded with seriousness. Instead of consenting to a subsequent discussion, she asked him to send her an email encompassing a concise overview of his opinions.

Balwani, Holmes's associate, issued an email in which he both insulted and threatened Shultz in his reply. Subsequently, he paid a visit to his grandfather, who held a position as a board member at Theranos. Nevertheless, his grandfather initially harbored doubts about his abilities. The situation reached its climax with a gathering at the home of Tyler Shultz's grandfather, during which Theranos lawyers successfully persuaded him to sign a confidentiality agreement. Previously, Tyler Shultz's family had counseled him to relinquish his association with the corporation but he disagreed. Similar to Shultz, Cheung experienced coercion from corporate lawyers. Cheung corresponded with the regulatory agency, Centers for Medicare & Medicaid Services (CMS), wherein she revealed the problems that were transpiring at the Theranos laboratory. Subsequently, the regulatory body carried out an impromptu examination of the start-up company's laboratories, during which several regulatory infractions were uncovered. During the intervening period, Tyler Shultz informed a journalist about the event instead of contacting the authorities. In an internal post written in October 2015,

He revealed that Theranos was not utilizing its proprietary devices for blood tests and that the "Edison" gadget yielded erroneous outcomes. Theranos refuted the charges, asserting their full falsehood, and warned of potential legal consequences for the journalist and Shultz.

CHAPTER FIVE

The Impact of Theranos Fraud Allegations

Walgreens temporarily halted its collaboration with Theranos, the pharmaceutical retail company. In January 2016, upon discovering that Theranos tests were unable to reliably detect a blood thinner, the state regulator CMS issued a warning indicating that Theranos testing constituted a risk to patient well-being. Following a further three-month period, the Securities and Exchange

Commission (SEC) and law enforcement initiated an investigation into Theranos. Balwani, who was responsible for overseeing the group's daily activities, made the decision to depart from the organization. The litigation initiated by Walgreens and its partners against Theranos in 2017 was ended through a settlement agreement between the parties.

In 2018, the Securities and Exchange Commission (SEC) lodged accusations against Elizabeth Holmes and her business associate Balwani. After being compelled to step down as CEO, Holmes faced a ten-year prohibition from assuming any management role in a publicly traded corporation. In June 2018, Holmes and Balwani were both indicted with criminal charges by California law enforcement. The group terminated its operations in September of the same year.

Erika Cheung and Tyler Shultz opted to expose the organization due to their perception that their grievances were not being adequately acknowledged. Cheung had sought out Balwani, the second-in-command at Theranos, to raise awareness about the company's mishandling of inaccurate test outcomes. Instead of approaching

Cheung with seriousness, he questioned her ability to successfully accomplish the appointed work. Theranos issued a legal threat against her after she resigned from the company due to her unhappiness.

Upon receiving Shultz's findings, Elizabeth Holmes, the CEO of the corporation, asked him to document his concerns. Despite possessing photographic evidence of the employee's misconduct, the employer opted to administer reprimands and engage in other retaliatory actions instead of initiating an inquiry. Balwani's email to Shultz contained both insults and threats. By employing this approach, Theranos successfully subverted a key element of efficient corporate adherence. This pillar represents a robust environment where employees are encouraged to voice their concerns or report wrongdoing without any apprehension of retaliation.

Additionally, a number of former employees came out, revealing the company's stringent culture of confidentiality. It was claimed that Holmes and Theranos President Ramesh "Sunny" Balwani were cognizant of the deficiencies in the technologies and that the Edison machines and tests were not adequately prepared for extensive public utilization. However, they compelled employees to fabricate testing data and conduct deceptive demonstrations of the machines to attract potential investors. Theranos attorneys also made threats towards other employees.

The Final Days of Theranos

The Food and Drug Administration and the Centers for Medicare & Medicaid Services (CMS), a regulatory body in the healthcare business, initiated investigations. The FDA declared in October 2015 that Theranos' "nanotainer" vial was an unapproved medical device. Subsequently, in January 2016, the CMS closed down Theranos' facility in Newark, California, due to an imminent threat to patient health and safety. Theranos closed its "Wellness Centers" and Balwani resigned as company president and COO by the end of the year. Investors incurred substantial financial losses, resulting in multiple lawsuits seeking compensation, including one filed by Walgreens.

Theranos reached a settlement with the CMS in April 2017. The corporation incurred a penalty of $30,000 and received a two-year prohibition from engaging in activities within the blood-testing sector. The company shifted its focus to manufacturing its technology rather than processing clinical samples. In that particular month, Theranos reached a resolution for a state fraud allegation, reimbursing a total of $4.6

million to individuals in Arizona who had utilized their testing services.

In March 2018, the Securities and Exchange Commission filed charges against Theranos, Holmes, and Balwani, alleging that they engaged in a substantial fraudulent scheme to secure over $700 million in funding. As part of her agreement with the SEC, Holmes did not confess to wrongdoing but instead paid a fine of $500,000, gave up her ability to control the majority of votes in Theranos, and was prohibited from assuming a leadership role in any publicly traded firm for a period of 10 years.

Following layoffs, several investigations, settlements, and significant changes in leadership—Balwani departed in 2016, and Holmes resigned as CEO in June 2018—CEO David Taylor declared on September 5, 2018, that Theranos would liquidate its assets in an effort to compensate creditors using its remaining funds.

CHAPTER SIX

Court Proceedings, and Penology

The trial of Holmes was the much-anticipated conclusion to the Theranos scandal, a company that was once valued at $9 billion and praised as groundbreaking. However, as more evidence emerged questioning the reliability of its blood-testing equipment, the company ultimately fell apart. The hearings also offered a critical analysis of the occasionally ambiguous boundaries between optimistic projections and blatant deception in technology start-ups, as venture capitalists invest unprecedented amounts of money into young yet potential enterprises. Theranos purported to be advancing technology that could perform a variety of medical tests with only a small amount of blood. The company reached an agreement to provide testing services to patients at Walgreens and secured a funding of over $700 million from investors, including investment firm DFJ, the Walton family of Walmart, and media tycoon Rupert Murdoch.

Nevertheless, the company's decline commenced following the publication of an article in 2015, which revealed that it had utilized non-branded diagnostic equipment instead of its own exclusive technology for conducting numerous tests. Three years later, the US justice department issued indictments against Holmes and Balwani, accusing them of intentionally deceiving doctors and patients while touting Theranos technology. Additionally, they were accused of misrepresenting the company's financial status and future prospects to investors. Balwani, Holmes, and Theranos had previously resolved allegations of fraud with the Securities and Exchange Commission. As part of the settlement, Holmes consented to pay a penalty of $500,000 and surrender her ownership in the company. The company disbanded and transferred its patents to Fortress Investment Group, one of its creditors.

Despite Holmes persistently refuting the accusations of fraud, a grand jury indicted her and Balwani on June 14, 2018, charging them with nine charges of wire fraud and two counts of conspiracy to commit wire fraud. The ultimate indictment, issued in July 2020, featured an extra charge of wire fraud. Each of them underwent separate trials in the federal court. In September

2021, Holmes' criminal trial commenced after being postponed twice owing to the COVID-19 epidemic and her first pregnancy. She entered a plea of not guilty and provided testimony for a duration of seven days throughout the 15-week trial.

On January 3, 2022, the jury rendered a verdict of guilt against Holmes on three counts of wire fraud, amounting to around $145 million in transactions, and one count of conspiracy to conduct wire fraud. Holmes was exonerated of four additional accusations, but the jury was unable to reach a verdict on the three remaining counts.

Testimony of Elizabeth Holmes

In late November, Holmes gave testimony, which surprised everyone. She alleged that, while a student at Stanford University, she experienced sexual assault, which led her to abandon her studies in order to pursue a career at Theranos. Holmes provided testimony over the course of seven days, asserting that her former lover Balwani had engaged in sexual assault and psychological abuse against her. Holmes and Balwani first encountered one other when Holmes was 18 years old, and subsequently, they maintained a relationship for a decade. Balwani is 20 years older than Holmes. Reportedly, he exerted control and condescension over every aspect of her life, including her dietary choices, family interactions, and decision-making authority at her profession. According to her, her attackers misinterpreted her statement when they accused her of providing them with inaccurate details on a military agreement. She admitted her remorse for the fabricated report that featured the brand logos.

Furthermore, she confessed to employing private detectives and lawyers to intimidate former employees, namely Erika Cheung and Tyler Shultz, who had exposed the illicit business practices. The defense repeatedly attempted to discredit the investigators by asserting that they mishandled the case. During the cross-examination, Holmes's attorneys consistently insinuated that the investors had compromised their thorough investigation process in order to swiftly generate profits. Companies such as Uber and WeWork entice investors with grandiose claims about their occasionally untested technologies, but they do not become profitable until several years into their operations.

The technique was based on the premise that in Silicon Valley, it is customary to make audacious assertions. Holmes's association with Balwani necessitated her to confess about an adulterous relationship she had with another individual while they were in a relationship. She was summoned to the witness stand to recite a collection of emails and text messages that she had corresponded with her former business associate regarding issues at Theranos. Upon considering the defense's assertions, the prosecution diligently endeavored to establish, with absolute certainty, that Holmes possessed full knowledge of all the misconduct within her organization.

At the end of her trial in December 2021, Holmes was convicted of four out of the eleven accusations brought against her, specifically for investment fraud. However, she was acquitted of other allegations, such as patient fraud. In the months preceding her sentence in October 2022, an unforeseen occurrence took place: a crucial witness paid a visit to her residence in August and conveyed remorse for his involvement in her incarceration. The postponement of her punishment was due to this.

Former Theranos lab director Adam Rosendorff initially professed sorrow, but eventually admitted in court to having consistently lied during the trial. Although Rosendorff visited Holmes's residence, the judge did not mandate a retrial, presumably to preempt Holmes from utilizing the incident as grounds for an appeal. In other words, the judge prohibited Holmes from utilizing the knowledge acquired during Rosendorff's visit to her residence.

In November 2022, Holmes received a prison sentence exceeding 11 years. The defense attorneys for Holmes had requested a sentence of 18 months of confinement at home; hence, this penalty was far more severe than the previous one. As a result of the arrival of her second child, Holmes has requested to be granted parole from prison while awaiting the decision of her appeal. The federal judge denied her plea for a postponement of her sentence, thereby requiring her to present herself to the correctional facility on April 27, 2023.

The verdict serves as a clear indication from the US government to Silicon Valley that founders must exercise greater caution in promoting the potential of their companies, despite the well-known challenges in successfully prosecuting white collar fraud cases in the United States. Henceforth, company founders will need to exercise greater prudence while promoting the capabilities of their products.

In November of that year, a judge in a U.S. federal court imposed a sentence of 11 years and three months of imprisonment on Holmes, to be followed by three years of supervised release. Both she and Balwani, who was convicted on all 12 crimes, are now have to pay $452 million in reparations. Holmes was released on bail and subsequently commenced her incarceration on May 30, 2023.

Association with Sunny Balwani

Holmes encountered Ramesh "Sunny" Balwani during her adolescence while she was pursuing her studies in China. Despite a significant age difference of almost two decades, the two individuals finally developed a personal relationship even prior to becoming business associates. In 2005, they began cohabitating, and when Balwani became a part of the company four years afterwards, they chose to conceal their romantic involvement from investors and the majority of staff.

In 2016, Balwani departed from Theranos, which at the time was deeply entangled in controversy. At this juncture, Holmes and Balwani's romantic relationship also terminated, prompting Holmes to relocate from their jointly inhabited residence.

During both her interview and testimony in her federal trial, Holmes has asserted that Balwani subjected her to emotional and sexual abuse. She stated that he expressed a tendency to be highly judgmental and exert excessive control over her dietary choices and daily routine, along with other instances of mistreatment. Due to these accusations, which Balwani's defense team refuted, the two individuals were tried separately despite being jointly indicted. Balwani was found guilty on all 12 counts and is currently serving a 13-year prison term.

In 2017, Holmes encountered and initiated a romantic relationship with entrepreneur Billy Evans, whose family has a hotel enterprise in San Diego. Despite the legal difficulties she was encountering, Holmes was married in June 2019 to Billy Evans, the inheritor of a hotel enterprise in California. In July 2021, she delivered their son, William and resided in California until Holmes' incarceration. The commencement of her criminal trial was postponed by a few weeks due to her pregnancy. The couple's daughter, Invicta, was born in February 2023. Visitation rights will be granted to her family to see Holmes in prison.

END

www.ingramcontent.com/pod-product-compliance
Lightning Source LLC
Chambersburg PA
CBHW071101260726
48661CB00006B/2390